To all grandmothers who will be completing this book,
I am five times lucky and will be filling in
five copies of this book as soon as it is published!
Lots of photographs to copy, hours
telling each newly-loved little person about my life....

And because I, and each one of us, don't have perfectly
conventional lives, I will cross out some of the headings
– and put beautiful letters from my sons and husband
over some of the pages that don't apply to my life.

I encourage you to change the book to fit your life –
some of you may have been divorced,
or may have adopted children.
Glue totally unsuitable pages together! Indeed,
glue in pages of special memorabilia and
cross out headings that don't work for you.
You can even glue a photograph of yourself over
this introduction. The *more* messed-up,
crossed out and personal your final gift is,
the more precious, the more genuine it will be.

Helen Exley

with love for

from

date

OTHER HELEN EXLEY GIFTBOOKS:

To a very special Grandma
The love between Grandmothers and Grandchildren
To a very special Granddaughter
To a very special Grandson
My daughter, My Joy
To my daughter with love – a mother remembers
(in the same size and format as this book)

Published in 2007 by Helen Exley Giftbooks in Great Britain.

ILLUSTRATED BY JULIETTE CLARKE
WRITTEN BY PAM BROWN AND HELEN EXLEY

My thanks to Pam Brown, your assistance was invaluable to me – Helen Exley
Dedicated with great love to Kezia, Jasper, Oskar, Kane and baby Rudi

2   4   6   8   10   12   11   9   7   5   3

Helen Exley Giftbooks, 16 Chalk Hill, Watford, Herts WD19 4BG, UK
www.helenexleygiftbooks.com

Grandmother Remembers

Written with love for my grandchild

A HELEN EXLEY GIFTBOOK

Contents

GREAT GRANDMOTHER	GREAT GRANDFATHER

GREAT GRANDMOTHER	GREAT GRANDFATHER

GRANDMOTHER	GRANDFATHER

Y ou are woven
from a thousand lives
– the family that came before you.
Each has given you a gift –
each has played
a part in what you are.

GREAT GRANDMOTHER

GREAT GRANDFATHER

GREAT GRANDMOTHER

GREAT GRANDFATHER

GRANDMOTHER

GRANDFATHER

MOTHER

FATHER

NAME

YOUR FAMILY TREE

There has never been anyone quite like you.
You took a little from everyone who came before you.

Look back, my love,
and see the procession
of your ancestors
– each handing on
their memories,
their dreams
– each now a part of you.

My grandparents

My Mother's Family

My grandparents' details

When and how they lived

My grandfather earned his living

Their talents

My Father's Family

My grandparents' details

When and how they lived

My grandfather earned his living

Their talents

Health history and important information

Things I've been told about them

When my grandparents lived

What I remember of them

_____

_____

Things I've been told about their lives and families

_____

_____

Living conditions for our family

_____

_____

How things were different for them

_____

New inventions and changes in their lifetime

_____

Great social changes and events in their time

_____

_____

Important events in their lives

_____

_____

How they spent their lives

_____

_____

_____

What opportunities existed for women?

Great achievements

Great losses

Important events

Other information about my grandparents

PHOTOGRAPHS OF MY GRANDPARENTS

OLD FAMILY PHOTOGRAPHS

History of my family

Earliest known history and origins of the family

Great historical events – wars, peace, natural disasters that affected our family

Social changes that affected us

Financial background and changes in our family

Important family events

Medical histories, causes of death

Occupations

Talents and achievements

Other stories and memories

The world when my mother was young

The great world events when she was a child

_____

_____

_____

_____

_____

How world events affected my mother and her family

_____

_____

_____

Great world events when she grew up

_____

_____

_____

_____

The medical advances and how they affected her life and world

_____

_____

_____

The great inventions in her life

_____

_____

_____

When radio, electricity, cars came...

Books/great people who changed her life

The political changes in her lifetime

My mother

Her maiden name

Why her first names were chosen

Her birth date, birthplace and important facts

Her education

Family life

Her greatest adventures

Her talents and skills

Stories she told

Her hopes, dreams and plans

The things she liked and disliked most

The things she feared most

Her hardest times

Her funniest memories

Her happiest times

Her greatest achievement/s

Other important facts and events

My father

Why his first names were chosen
_____

His birth date, his birthplace and important facts
_____
_____

His education
_____
_____

His greatest achievements
_____
_____

His greatest disappointments
_____
_____

His talents and skills
_____
_____
_____

His hopes, dreams, plans
_____
_____

Things he liked and disliked most
_____
_____

Things he feared
_____
_____

His hardest times
_____
_____
_____

His happiest times
_____
_____

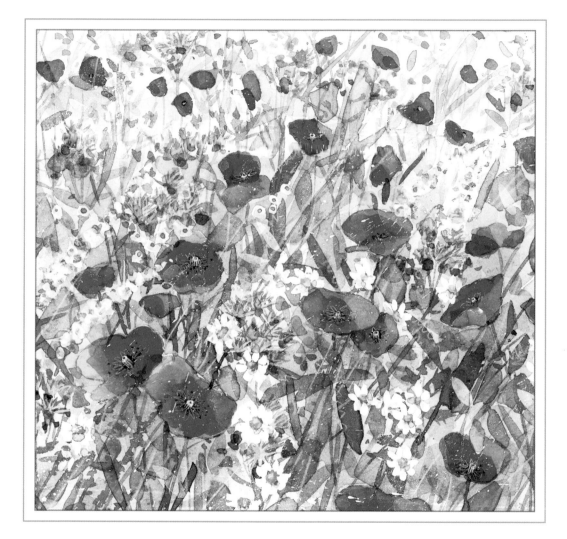

His funniest stories/memories

Other important and interesting things

PHOTOGRAPHS OF MY MOTHER

Becoming a woman

My mother's best stories about growing up – as a woman

The barriers most women faced

The obstacles she faced

The dreams...

What she has overcome as a woman

What she taught me about my role

How things have changed for women as I grew up

What obstacles remained for me

My successes and failures

My parents' wedding

My parents' wedding day

How my parents met

Stories they have told of their romance and courtship

What my mother told me about her wedding day

Marriage and home

Where my parents lived

What their home/s looked like

Their financial state

Their struggles

Their successes

What occupation/s they had

What they liked about each other

How world events affected their lives

What I have heard of their life together

Stories about the family – and special memories

PHOTOGRAPH OF ME AS A CHILD

Me!

The names I was given when I was born

The reason for those names

My pet names, my nicknames

Important facts

Memories of when I was very young

What I disliked and feared

Stories about me as a baby

Stories about me as a child

The best of my memories

Memories of my childhood

Our family

Brothers, sisters, and relations

Early adventures

Sad times

Happy times

Things that formed my character

My first loves – flowers, books, animals...

My early talents

Things I most disliked

Things that hadn't been invented then

Things about me then that changed a lot

Things I'll never forget

PHOTOGRAPHS OF ME AS A CHILD

My school days

My best subjects
_____

School work I most disliked
_____

My talents and achievements
_____

How I got to school
_____

What school was like when I was young
_____

What is better at schools today
_____

What is worse in schools today
_____

What were school rules that aren't here today
_____

What was discipline like then
_____

What made me laugh
_____

Memories you would like to hear
_____
_____
_____

PHOTOGRAPH OF ME AT SCHOOL

When I was young

The first sight of the sea

Learning to swim/play sport

My first dance

Music, books that I loved

Travel memories

First successes

My early failures

My best memories

My early strong values and beliefs

A PHOTOGRAPH OF ME AS A TEENAGER AND YOUNG WOMAN

My first passions and major interests

Other special firsts

My dreams

What I dreamed about

People, books, events, music that made me dream

What I wanted to be

My hopes for the world and what I believed in

My concerns – political, social, personal

Anxiety and excitements about growing up

Broken dreams

Dreams that have stayed with me

Love and romance

How I met your grandad

What I remember about falling in love

What I most liked about him

What he most liked about me

Romantic moments

Our song, our special places

The things we did together

Some obstacles and problems we overcame

Unforgettable memories

Our hopes and dreams

A PHOTOGRAPH OF YOUR GRANDAD AND ME

My wedding

The date and place of our wedding

Your grandfather's full name

About him – his life, his work, his family

What the wedding was like – my dress, the reception, the music and all the details

Description of my special, my lovely, day

Things that went wrong!

My happiest memories

PHOTOGRAPHS OF OUR WEDDING

$\mathcal{A}$nything, everything, little or big, becomes an adventure when the right person shares it.

KATHLEEN NORRIS (1880-1966)

PHOTOGRAPH/S OF OUR EARLY LIFE TOGETHER

Early times together

What we grew to love about each other

Where we lived, what our first homes were like

Practical early problems

How we overcame problems

Building a family

Things we bought that I still treasure

Sad memories

Wonderful memories

Your parent is born!

Your parent's birth details

Why we chose his/her first names

What/who he/she looked like

The first thoughts I had

Worrying things

Happy times

Practical problems of babies in those days

What I loved about him/her

My strongest memories

PHOTOGRAPHS OF MY CHILD – YOUR MOTHER OR FATHER

Your parent growing up

Going to school

The funniest things!

Naughty days!

Talents

Hobbies and interests

Early dreams

Greatest achievements

...and interests

What has made me most proud

A PHOTOGRAPH OF ME AND YOUR PARENT

Me and your parent

The connection I have felt

How he/she changed my life

What I've learned from him/her

What we have in common

Ways in which we are utterly different

What has made me laugh/happy

Our strengths together

Sorrows we've shared

Things we both enjoyed doing together

You!

My memories of the first time I saw you

My hopes and fears for you when you were born

How your birth changed my life

The world you were born into... world events and changes

Things that are very different to my childhood

PHOTOGRAPHS OF ME AND YOU

PHOTOGRAPHS OF YOU

You – the early years

What I thought of you

_____

Things that made me laugh

_____

What made me proud

_____

_____

Funny things you did or said

_____

_____

Things you loved

_____

What we loved

_____

_____

What frightened you and calmed you

_____

_____

_____

My happiest memories

_____

_____

_____

PHOTOGRAPHS OF GIRLS AT MY TIME – OR ME

How the world has changed in my lifetime

Inventions

Household chores when I was young

Population growth and how it has changed our town, nature, shopping...

Medical cures

Transport changes

What we did for fun

The coming of television and changes to radio

Major world events that have affected my life, my family

Changes in society's values

Other important changes

Sad things

The great personal sorrows of my life

_____

_____

_____

_____

About beloved people I remember

_____

_____

_____

Major events: wars, epidemics, natural disasters

_____

_____

_____

_____

Things that worry me and my fears for your world

_____

_____

_____

My feelings of sadness and disappointment about the world

_____

_____

_____

_____

My beliefs, my passions

Important beliefs that have inspired my life

The great teachers

The great political leaders

Other "ordinary", very extraordinary, people in my life

Books that have changed my life

Great movies

Great artists...

Historical changes and events that have affected/changed me

Central events in my own life that have changed me

Things I have loved

Things I have loved

_____

Movies/Shows

_____

Music, songs

_____

Pets and animals

_____

Food

_____

Flowers, trees, nature

_____

Places, countries

_____

Hobbies and activities

_____

Things I'd like to share with you

_____

The most-loved, glorious memories of my life…

I have such hopes for you – not fame or riches, though they may come, but the enthusiasm to make bold choices, to learn and experiment and make and do. To weather storms. To learn from failure. To discover goodness in other people.

Words by Pam Brown, B.1928

A PHOTOGRAPH OF YOU AND ME TOGETHER

My hopes for you

I wish you the joy of this music I have loved

I wish you these extraordinary sights

…these books, these movies

…these special places

…moments of this kind of special love

Adventures I wish you

Things I wish I'd learned

Things I've never done, risks I've never taken that I hope you'll have the courage to

Other loves I wish you

Letters, copies of documents, photographs –
extra space for everything else that's important

Other important extras

For your choice of press cuttings, personal thoughts,
a loved poem, a special picture....

*T*ake with you into your future all my love.

All the things we've seen together,

all the music we've heard,

all the people we have met and loved,

all the secrets, all the gigglings,

all the mischiefs we have made.

I'll come with you as far as I'm allowed

along your road –

and when we part you'll take with you

my hopes and half my heart.

Words by Pam Brown, B.1928

A letter from me to you